A LITTLE
GOD
TIME

FOR
Women

DEVOTIONAL
COLORING
BOOK

BroadStreet
PUBLISHING

BroadStreet Publishing®
Savage, Minnesota, USA

Majestic Expressions is an imprint of BroadStreet Publishing Group, LLC.
Broadstreetpublishing.com

A Little God Time for Women *(Devotional Coloring Book)*
© 2024 by BroadStreet Publishing®

9781424569243

Typesetting and design by Garborg Design Works | garborgdesign.com
Compiled and edited by Michelle Winger | literallyprecise.com

Printed in China.

24 25 26 27 28 29 30   7 6 5 4 3 2 1

Introduction

Life is full of demands. Appointments, deadlines, obligations, and constant digital chatter occupy every moment and build a mountain of unhealthy stress and tension. Coloring is an effective stress reducer, but true rest and peace are found in God.

A Little God Time for Women perfectly combines encouraging devotions and inspiring illustrations in one beautiful book. Spend time reflecting on the truth of God's Word and be filled with his joy and peace. Express your creativity freely as you fill the intricate images with the beauty of color.

Take a break from your busy schedule and the stress that accompanies it. The worries of life can wait.

The Father's Love

"If a man has a hundred sheep but one of the sheep gets lost, he will leave the other ninety-nine on the hill and go to look for the lost sheep. I tell you the truth, if he finds it he is happier about that one sheep than about the ninety-nine that were never lost."

MATTHEW 18:12-13 NCV

Regardless of how beautifully or imperfectly your earthly father showed his love, your heavenly Father's love is utterly boundless. Rest in that thought a moment. There is nothing you can do to change how he feels about you. *Nothing.*

We spend so much time trying to make ourselves more lovable, from beauty treatments to gourmet baking, to being there for pretty much everyone. It's easy to forget we are already perfectly loved.

Our Father loves us more than we can imagine. And he would do anything for us. *Anything.*

Who do you love most fiercely, most protectively, most desperately here on earth? What would you do for them? Know that it's a mere fraction, nearly immeasurable, of what God would do for you.

Father, thank you for loving me just as I am. Your love is extravagant and doesn't change depending on how I act, think, or feel. You are a perfect Father, and I love you.

Follow the Arrow

Your ears shall hear a word behind you, saying,
"This is the way, walk in it,"
Whenever you turn to the right hand
or whenever you turn to the left."

Isaiah 30:21 NKJV

Decisions, decisions. It seems a week never goes by without our needing to make at least one important choice.

Whether job related, relationship motivated, or something as seemingly innocent as how to spend a free Friday, wouldn't it be nice to have an arrow pointing us in the right direction—especially if we are in danger of making a wrong turn?

According to the Word, we have exactly that. When we truly desire to walk the path God sets us on, and when we earnestly seek his voice, he promises to lead us in the right direction. His ever-present Spirit is right there, ready to put us back on the path each time we wander off.

Consider the decisions before you right now. Who are you turning to for guidance? Lay your options before God, and then listen for his voice.

God, there are so many decisions that I make each day. Some don't seem to matter, and others could be life changing. Help me to come to you first for guidance in all areas of my life. You care about each detail, and you can show me which way to turn.

You Are Perfect

By a single offering he has perfected for all time
those who are being sanctified.

Hebrews 10:14 ESV

You are perfect. Stop, go back, and read that again. *You are perfect.* Looking in the mirror, or thinking back over your day, it is easy to forget or disbelieve those words. Don't let that happen.

A wrinkle here, a bulge there, an unkind word, or a jealous thought cannot change the way the Father sees you. And it's how he wants you to see yourself.

The dictionary uses 258 words to explain what it means to be perfect, but we only need to know this: we are complete. When he chose to die on the cross for our sins, Jesus took away every flaw from those of us who love him and ask for his forgiveness. He finished what we never could, and he made us perfect.

Stand before a mirror and ask God to show you what he sees when he looks at you. See past the flaws, past any hurt or anger in your eyes, past any perceived imperfection. See yourself complete, just as you were meant to be. See yourself as perfect. How does this change the way you feel?

Lord, when I reflect on my imperfections, it can be overwhelming and depressing. Thank you that you see me for who I really am, and who I am meant to be. You have made me perfect through your sacrifice and I choose to walk in that today.

Cherished

I am convinced that neither death nor life, neither angels nor demons, neither the present nor the future, nor any powers, neither height nor depth, nor anything else in all creation, will be able to separate us from the love of God that is in Christ Jesus our Lord.

Romans 8:38-39 NIV

It's good to be loved, isn't it? What feeling really compares to knowing someone has run through the rain, cancelled an international flight, driven all night—for you? Even if we've never experienced it, we've imagined it in our hearts. Or else we've had the realization that we too would move heaven and earth for the one we love the most.

Whether husband, child, parent, sibling, or dear friend, to love and be loved deeply just may be the best feeling there is.

How much love you have given or received is a mere sampling of the way Jesus feels about you. You are cherished, loved beyond reason or measure. The one who really can move heaven and earth would do so in a heartbeat—for you.

Let the incredible words above wash over you as you realize there is nothing, absolutely nothing, Jesus wouldn't do for you. Can you feel his love toward you today?

God, I feel your love today. You sacrificed everything to show me that you cherish me. You want to spend time with me. You delight in me. I bask in your love today and choose to let it fill me, so I am overflowing with love for you and others.

Troubled Heart

"Peace I leave with you; my peace I give you. I do not give to you as the world gives. Do not let your hearts be troubled and do not be afraid."

JOHN 14:27 NIV

I can't get a moment's peace. Sound familiar? We all go through seasons where it seems every corner hides a new challenge to our serenity, assuming we've actually achieved any semblance of serenity in the first place. Why is it so hard to find peace in this world? Because we're looking in this world.

After his resurrection before Jesus ascended into heaven, he left his disciples with something they'd never had before: peace. More specifically, he gave them his peace, a gift not of this world.

Whatever the world can offer us can also be taken from us. Any security, happiness, or temporary reprieve from suffering is just that: temporary. Only the things of heaven are permanent and cannot be taken away.

Do not let your heart be troubled, Jesus tells us. This means we have a choice. Share the things with him that threaten your peace, and then remember they have no hold on you. You are his, and his peace is yours. How can you choose peace in your situation today?

Father, so many things threaten to take my peace every day. Thank you that your peace can be my peace when I choose it. I don't want my heart to be troubled, so help me give up the thoughts that are causing unrest.

Peace I leave with you; my peace I give you.

John 14:27 NIV

The Patience Pit

I waited and waited and waited some more,
patiently, knowing God would come through for me.
Then, at last, he bent down and listened to my cry.

PSALM 40:1 TPT

We're not that good at waiting for anything these days. Yet the reality is that waiting is a necessary part of life. We wait for people, we wait for events, and we wait for desires to be fulfilled. But do we recognize that waiting might also apply to our emotional lives? Do we hold on to hope that we can be rescued from a troubled heart?

King David described himself as being in a pit of miry clay, likely another of his despairing moments perhaps even on reflection of his sins. He needed to be rescued, not necessarily from his enemies, but from his state of mind.

David says he waited patiently, understanding that he might not be instantly rescued. And he trusted that God alone would s ave him.

Do you feel as though your emotions are on slippery ground or that your thoughts are stuck in the miry clay? Are you willing to wait patiently for the great rescuer to lift you up and place your feet on solid ground? Take a moment today to ask God for his help.

God, sometimes I feel like you so far away. But in your Word you tell me that you are always near; you never leave me. I believe that today. I ask for your help and say that I will wait patiently for it. You will not disappoint me.

Creatures of Habit

Do not conform to the pattern of this world, but be transformed by the renewing of your mind. Then you will be able to test and approve what God's will is—his good, pleasing and perfect will.

ROMANS 12:2 NIV

Wake up. Make bed. Get dressed. Coffee. Not always in that order, but you can guarantee that many do those things every single morning. They might also bite their nails, anger easily, and stay up too late. Patterns are hard to break. We are, after all, creatures of habit, and unfortunately not all of those habits are good.

What do you do when you are confronted with a habit that is not positive? Do you recognize when you rely on something just because it makes you feel accepted, comforted, or in control? Sometimes we aren't even conscious of our habits until we try to give them up.

Scripture says that establishing the right pattern begins with the renewing of our minds. This means that we must first acknowledge the need for change, and then submit our way of thinking to resemble that of Christ.

What habits do you find yourself constantly trying to break? Can you trust God today to show you his good, pleasing, and perfect will as you submit your worldly patterns to him?

Father, I do have worldly patterns and habits that are hard to break. Help me to see your good, pleasing, and perfect will for my life and walk according to that each day.

Meditate on Goodness

Whatever is true, whatever is honorable, whatever is right, whatever is pure, whatever is lovely, whatever is of good repute, if there is any excellence and if anything worthy of praise, dwell on these things.

PHILIPPIANS 4:8 NASB

Do you ever catch yourself dwelling on the negative aspects of life? We can be indifferent when someone tells us good news, but talk for hours about conflict, worries, and disappointment.

It is good to communicate things that aren't going so well in our lives, but we can also fall into the trap of setting our minds on the wrong things.

Paul saw the need to address this within the church of Philippi. It seems there were people in the church that thought too highly of themselves and allowed discord to reside in their midst. Think of what dwelling on the negative actually does: it creates feelings of hopelessness, discouragement, and a lack of trust in our God who is good, true, and just.

Can you find anything in your life and the lives of others that have virtue or are worthy of praise? Choose to dwell on the true, noble, just, pure, and lovely things, and experience the refreshing nature of a positive outlook.

Father God, sometimes it's easier to be negative than positive. It's easy to look at everything that is going wrong and forget about all that is good. Help me to shift my focus and start seeing all of the excellence around me. You have truly blessed me with goodness.

Fully Trusting

Trust in the LORD with all your heart,
And lean not on your own understanding;
In all your ways acknowledge Him,
And He shall direct your paths.

Proverbs 3:5-6 NKJV

Trust can be a hard word to put into action mostly because our experience with others tells us that we can be sorely disappointed. People let us down in many ways. We can even be disappointed in ourselves.

Remember the trust game that involved standing with eyes closed and falling back into the hands of a few peers in hopes that they would catch you? There was risk involved in that game, and it didn't always turn out well. Nothing can truly be guaranteed in this life, can it? Well, it depends on where you place your trust.

God watches over us, cares for us, and is involved in our lives. When we acknowledge that every good thing comes from him, our faith is strengthened, and we are able to trust him more. Make a point of noticing how God directs your paths today and thank him for being trustworthy.

Trust doesn't come easy, God. When I think about it, it seems crazy that I withhold trust from you—the one who created me and knows me intimately! I choose today to look at all the good places you have led me and continue to lead me. You are trustworthy and I thank you for that.

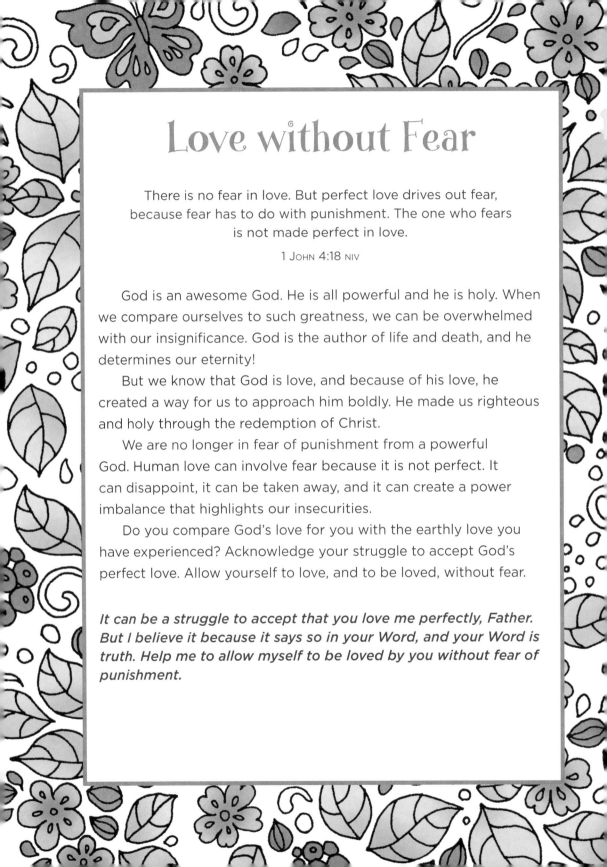

Love without Fear

There is no fear in love. But perfect love drives out fear, because fear has to do with punishment. The one who fears is not made perfect in love.

1 John 4:18 niv

God is an awesome God. He is all powerful and he is holy. When we compare ourselves to such greatness, we can be overwhelmed with our insignificance. God is the author of life and death, and he determines our eternity!

But we know that God is love, and because of his love, he created a way for us to approach him boldly. He made us righteous and holy through the redemption of Christ.

We are no longer in fear of punishment from a powerful God. Human love can involve fear because it is not perfect. It can disappoint, it can be taken away, and it can create a power imbalance that highlights our insecurities.

Do you compare God's love for you with the earthly love you have experienced? Acknowledge your struggle to accept God's perfect love. Allow yourself to love, and to be loved, without fear.

It can be a struggle to accept that you love me perfectly, Father. But I believe it because it says so in your Word, and your Word is truth. Help me to allow myself to be loved by you without fear of punishment.

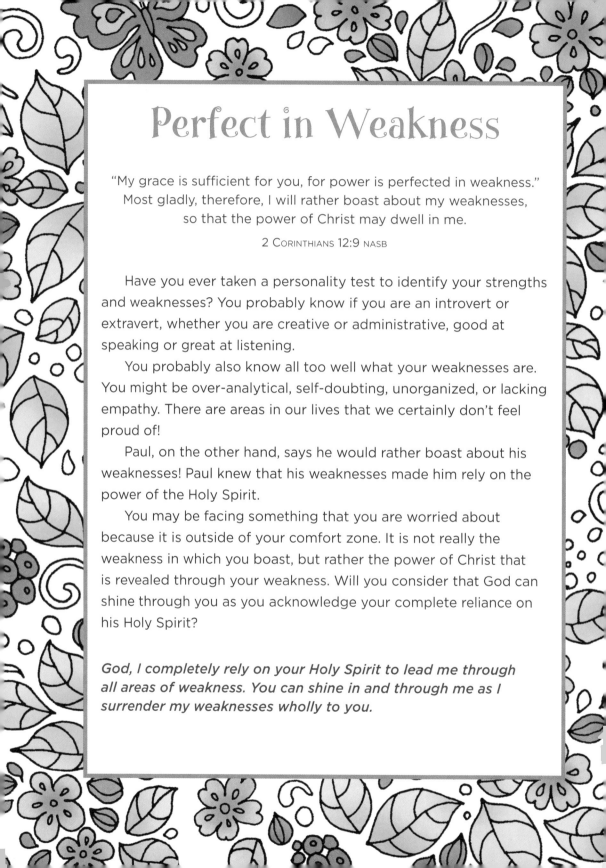

Perfect in Weakness

"My grace is sufficient for you, for power is perfected in weakness."
Most gladly, therefore, I will rather boast about my weaknesses,
so that the power of Christ may dwell in me.

2 CORINTHIANS 12:9 NASB

Have you ever taken a personality test to identify your strengths and weaknesses? You probably know if you are an introvert or extravert, whether you are creative or administrative, good at speaking or great at listening.

You probably also know all too well what your weaknesses are. You might be over-analytical, self-doubting, unorganized, or lacking empathy. There are areas in our lives that we certainly don't feel proud of!

Paul, on the other hand, says he would rather boast about his weaknesses! Paul knew that his weaknesses made him rely on the power of the Holy Spirit.

You may be facing something that you are worried about because it is outside of your comfort zone. It is not really the weakness in which you boast, but rather the power of Christ that is revealed through your weakness. Will you consider that God can shine through you as you acknowledge your complete reliance on his Holy Spirit?

God, I completely rely on your Holy Spirit to lead me through all areas of weakness. You can shine in and through me as I surrender my weaknesses wholly to you.

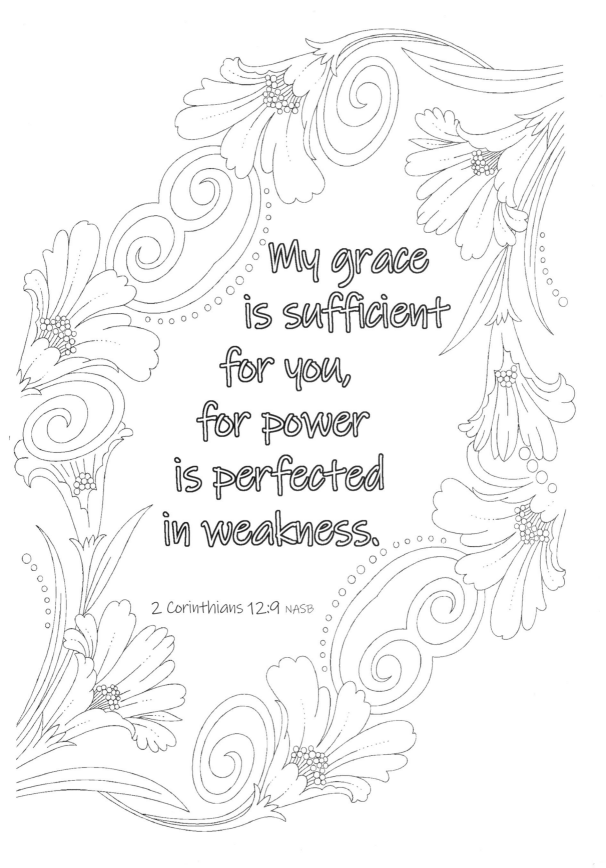

My grace
is sufficient
for you,
for power
is perfected
in weakness.

2 Corinthians 12:9 NASB

Comparison

Let each person examine his own work, and then he can
take pride in himself alone, and not compare himself
with someone else.

GALATIANS 6:4 CSB

In the age of social media, comparison has become an easier default than it's ever been before. When every image we see of others has been properly angled, edited, filtered, and cropped, we are quickly led into the delusion that the lives we see portrayed in those images are perfect.

We believe that the smiling faces we see in that post are always smiling, and the perfect homes with the beautiful lighting are permanently well-kept and polished.

The danger of these filtered images is that we end up comparing ourselves to something that isn't an accurate standard. What we don't see is the life outside that frame. We don't see the mess, the struggles, and the imperfections that are inevitably part of every life—even the perfect-looking ones.

God wants you to be so invested in the work that he has given you to do that you are not distracted or dissatisfied by what you see someone else doing. What does your unique lifestyle look like?

God, I dive headfirst into my uniqueness. I say yes to contentment and joy and move forward into greater fulfillment and happiness because you have chosen me to be just who I am. No more comparisons, God!

Impossible

Behold, I will do a new thing,
Now it shall spring forth;
Shall you not know it?
I will even make a road in the wilderness
And rivers in the desert.

Isaiah 43:19 NKJV

What seems impossible to you today? What have you given up on, walked away from, and written off as absurd? What dreams have you let die simply because you felt they were unattainable?

Maybe our dreams, though they seem far off, were placed in our hearts for a purpose. And maybe they won't look exactly the way we always thought they would, but maybe they'll still come true in a new way.

Maybe the things that seem insurmountable to us will be easily overcome when we simply shift perspective and look at them differently.

Beloved, you serve a God who is powerful enough to make a path appear right through an empty wilderness and create a stream of lifegiving water in the middle of a desert. He is more than able to take even the most impossible of situations and provide clarity, direction, and the means to make it through.

God, I trust you with my impossibilities and rely on your strength for my weaknesses. I know you can make a way through my difficult circumstances.

Fully Alive

When there is no clear prophetic vision,
people quickly wander astray.
But when you follow the revelation of the Word,
heaven's bliss fills your soul.

Proverbs 29:18 TPT

Everyday living can suck the life right out of us. Somewhere in the middle of being stuck in traffic, sweeping floors, and brushing our teeth, we can forget to be alive.

What does it mean to be alive, rather than just to live? Not to only exist in life, but to know it, to understand it, to experience it—to *live* it. What would it be like? Freefalling from an airplane. Running through the grass barefoot with sun on your face. Bringing babies into the world, screaming and strong with power and life.

What would it be like if we lived each moment in the spirit of those fully alive moments?

Without a reason for life, without purpose, we perish. We falter. We lose our way. We lose hope. We begin to casually exist instead of breathing in the reverence of a fully alive life. What dreams has God given you that you've lost along the way?

God, I trust that the dreams you gave me and I've somehow lost will be returned to me. You breathed life into me so that I could live to the fullest. I want that too.

A Way Out

No temptation has overtaken you except what is common to mankind. And God is faithful; he will not let you be tempted beyond what you can bear. But when you are tempted, he will also provide a way out so that you can endure it.

1 Corinthians 10:13 niv

Each of us struggles with temptation. No one is exempt. From gossip to overindulging, to unkind thoughts and more, we battle with temptation in all different ways.

The good news is that we serve a God who is faithful, and, oh, how he loves his children! The Bible tells us that he won't allow us to be faced with more than what we can handle. When we turn to him in the middle of our struggles, we can find our way out.

Be prepared for your time of battle by praying for protection. Ask the Lord to open your eyes to see the ways in which you may fall, so that you can be ready to face them head on.

Though temptation will surely come your way, be assured that it will not overcome you as you trust in the Lord.

God, when the way out of temptation doesn't seem clear, give me your eyes. I know I am blinded by the world in moments of struggle, and I need you to reach down, grab my hand, and lead me to the emergency exit. I trust you to help me.

He Hears

This is the confidence we have in approaching God:
that if we ask anything according to his will, he hears us.
And if we know that he hears us—whatever we ask—
we know that we have what we asked of him.

1 John 5:14-15 niv

Sometimes it feels like God is far away. Surely he cannot be interested in our day-to-day lives. Our desires and requests seem small; why would we ask him for help? But he is a God who loves his children. He wants us to be happy, to feel fulfilled.

The best way to know if something is true or right, is to hear it for yourself—straight from the source. You believe you nailed the interview, but you don't believe you got the job until you get the phone call. The same is true for bad news, at least ideally. You get wind of a rumor about a friend's indiscretion, but you wait for her side of the story before believing a word.

So what about God? How can we hear from him? How do we discern his will for our lives? We may not have a hotline, but we do have his book. God speaks to us through his Word, so if you are waiting for confirmation, direction, validation, or conviction, pick it up.

Allow yourself to be filled with God's presence. He loves you and wants the best for you.

Father God, you really do hear me. You tell me I can have confidence approaching you when I ask for your will in my life because you listen. Your blessings are abundant, and your grace is sufficient.

Rest Secure

I keep my eyes always on the LORD.
With him at my right hand, I will not be shaken.
Therefore my heart is glad and my tongue rejoices;
my body also will rest secure.

PSALM 16:8-9 NIV

A loud crash in the night. Unexpected footsteps uncomfortably close in a dark parking lot. A ringing phone at three o'clock in the morning. No matter how brave we think we are, certain situations quicken the pulse. We've heard over and over that we have nothing to fear if we walk with God, but let's be honest: certain situations are scary! So what does it mean to rest secure in the Lord?

No matter where you are, God is there too. While there may be times we ache to hide from him in our shame, he is a constant presence. The beautiful thing about his omnipresence is that we have a steady and consistent companion who is always ready to help in times of trouble.

We have no reason to fear the things that the world may throw our way. We've got the best protector of all at our side! Are you asking for his help in times of worry and woe, or are you turning inward to try to solve your problems?

Let God be your refuge. Nothing is too big or too small for him! Even in your darkest hours, you can know true joy because he is your guardian.

God, when I look to the world for comfort and encouragement, I come up empty. Nothing can fill me or protect me like you can. You are by my side, and you make me glad.

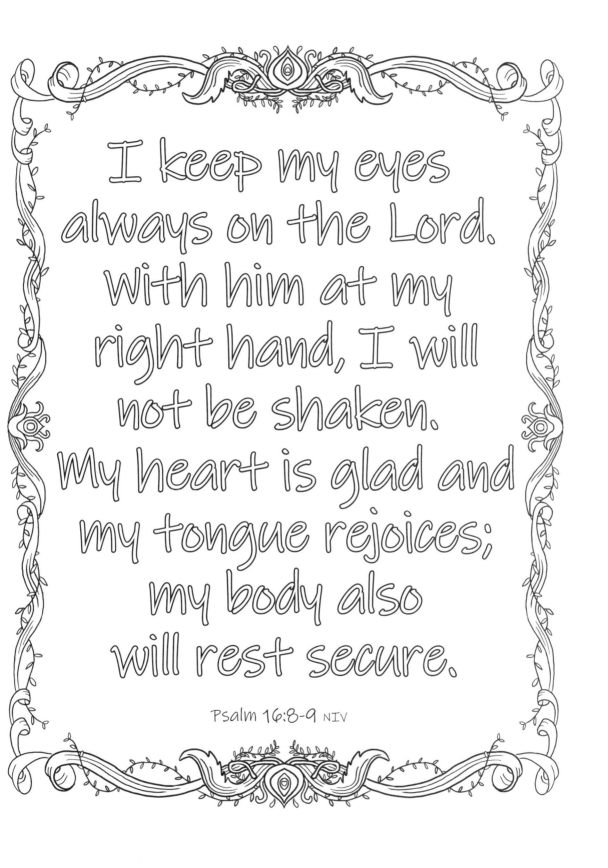

I keep my eyes
always on the Lord.
With him at my
right hand, I will
not be shaken.
My heart is glad and
my tongue rejoices;
my body also
will rest secure.

Psalm 16:8-9 NIV

Melody of Worship

The heavens declare the glory of God,
and the expanse proclaims the work of his hands.
Day after day they pour out speech,
night after night they communicate knowledge.

PSALM 19:1-2 CSB

Have you ever felt the song of your heart praising the Lord? No words may come, no verses, no chorus, and yet your very being feels as though it may burst from the music inside you. You are not alone! Even the heavens praise him in this way!

The Bible tells us that without words and without even the slightest sound, the skies burst forth in a song of praise for the glory of God. Isn't that an amazing picture? Can't you just envision an orchestra above you?

Break forth into your song! Allow your heart to feel the words, even if you cannot fully form them. Give God all your praises today. He is so deserving of them! Let your heart be a celebration of your love for Jesus Christ. Give in to the melody of worship inside you.

Father, regardless of how my voice sounds to others, when I pour out my worship before you, you hear a beautiful melody—a masterpiece even! I sing my song of praise to you today because you are worthy of all praise.

Unfailing Goodness

"I am now going the way of the whole earth, and you know with all your heart and all your soul that none of the good promises the LORD your God made to you has failed. Everything was fulfilled for you; not one promise has failed."

JOSHUA 23:14 CSB

Do you remember the first thing that you failed at? Maybe it was a test at school, a diet, a job interview, or even a relationship. Failure is difficult to admit especially in a culture that values outward success and appearance.

We often hear it said that success comes from many failures, but we only really hear that from successful people!

When Joshua was advanced in years, he reminded the Israelites of all that God had done for them. Though they had been unfaithful to God many times, God remained faithful, and they became a great nation that none could withstand.

God had a plan and a purpose for the nation of Israel, and through his power and mercy he ensured that these plans succeeded. In the same way, God has a purpose for your life, and while you may fail, he will not.

God, I take the opportunity today to submit my heart to your will. Not one good thing that you have planned for me will fail. Not one.

Eternal Fountain

"Whoever drinks of the water that I shall give him will never thirst. But the water that I shall give him will become in him a fountain of water springing up into everlasting life."

JOHN 4:14 NKJV

We take it for granted that when we turn on a faucet, water will come out. If we need something to drink, we can quench our thirst pretty easily. In Jesus' day however, people (usually women) had to get their water from the well often situated quite a walk away from their homes. It was a necessary daily task that provided for the family's needs.

Imagine being offered water that would last forever. This is what Jesus offered the woman at the well. She would never have to make this trip again in the heat of the day. She wanted this answer to her need.

Jesus compared the woman's desire with a spiritual desire: just as the well was a source for physical life, he was the source for eternal life.

You have received Jesus as the source for your life. Not only does Jesus say that he will provide you with everlasting water, but he also says that his water will be like a fountain springing up in you.

Father, I am so thankful for the eternal life that you have placed within me. I draw from you as my source of life today.

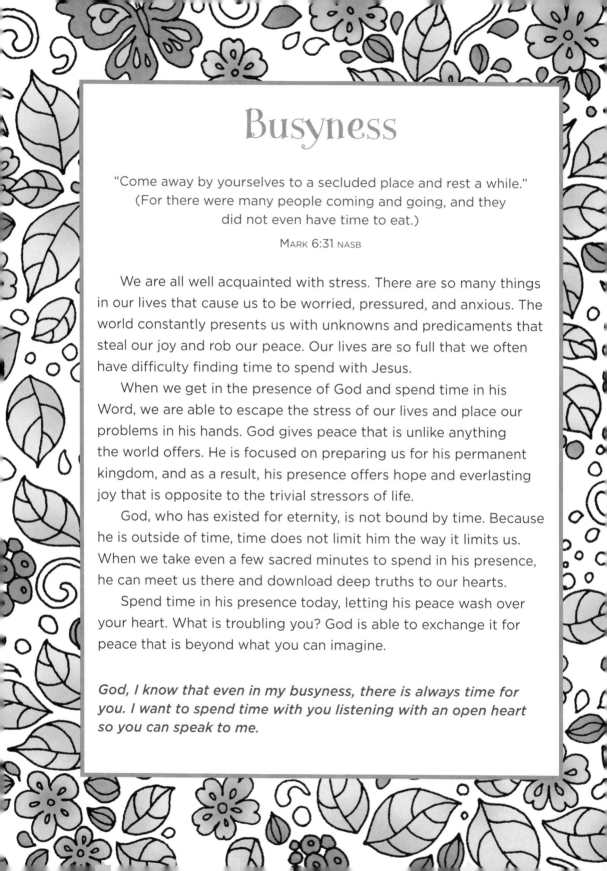

Busyness

"Come away by yourselves to a secluded place and rest a while."
(For there were many people coming and going, and they
did not even have time to eat.)

MARK 6:31 NASB

We are all well acquainted with stress. There are so many things in our lives that cause us to be worried, pressured, and anxious. The world constantly presents us with unknowns and predicaments that steal our joy and rob our peace. Our lives are so full that we often have difficulty finding time to spend with Jesus.

When we get in the presence of God and spend time in his Word, we are able to escape the stress of our lives and place our problems in his hands. God gives peace that is unlike anything the world offers. He is focused on preparing us for his permanent kingdom, and as a result, his presence offers hope and everlasting joy that is opposite to the trivial stressors of life.

God, who has existed for eternity, is not bound by time. Because he is outside of time, time does not limit him the way it limits us. When we take even a few sacred minutes to spend in his presence, he can meet us there and download deep truths to our hearts.

Spend time in his presence today, letting his peace wash over your heart. What is troubling you? God is able to exchange it for peace that is beyond what you can imagine.

God, I know that even in my busyness, there is always time for you. I want to spend time with you listening with an open heart so you can speak to me.

Living Word

The word of God is living and active, and sharper than any
two-edged sword, even penetrating as far as the division of soul
and spirit, of both joints and marrow, and able to judge the thoughts
and intentions of the heart.

HEBREWS 4:12 NASB

Have you ever noticed God speaking to you in themes? We all
go through different seasons in life, and God speaks to our hearts
accordingly. Some of us may be going through a season of learning
to wait, while another is learning how to step out in faith.

The beautiful thing about God is that he is big enough to speak
to all of us—in our different places, with our different hearts—at the
same time, with the same words.

God's Word is alive and active. It can deliver truth to the heart
of each person. Two people can get something completely different
from the same passage of Scripture because of what God has
been doing in each of their hearts separately. Through the body of
Christ, we can come together and share what God is teaching us,
multiplying our individual growth as we encourage one another.

Never doubt the power of what you hold in your hands when
you read the Word of God. Your Creator knows you so intimately
because he is the one who handcrafted your soul.

*Thank you, Father, that you care about me enough to speak
directly to my heart through your living Word. I want to hear
what you have to say to me today.*

Sand Castles

"Don't store up for yourselves treasures on earth, where moth and rust destroy and where thieves break in and steal. But store up for yourselves treasures in heaven, where neither moth nor rust destroys, and where thieves don't break in and steal. For where your treasure is, there your heart will be also."

MATTHEW 6:19-21 CSB

Have you ever been sitting on a beach and watched a little child work tirelessly on an elaborate sand castle? They spend hours perfecting their creation, thoughtfully forming each section, often stepping back to admire their work.

These little children are unaware of the patterns of ocean waves and don't realize that as the day passes, their masterpieces will eventually be swept away by the swelling tide. All that work, all that concentration, all that pride, gone as the water erases the shore.

What proverbial castles are we building in our lives that could, at any moment, be simply erased? We've got to buy into the bigger vision. We must know what can last and what won't. There are temporary kingdoms and a kingdom that will never pass away. We have to recognize which one we are contributing to.

If your work and your heart are invested in a heavenly vision, then what you have spent your life on will continue to matter for longer than you live. Where is your treasure today?

Father, I want to spend my time investing in the eternal souls of people, in the eternal vision of advancing your kingdom, and in the never-ending truth of the Gospel. In these things, I will find purpose and treasure that will never be lost.

Where your treasure is, there your heart will be also.

Matthew 6:21 CSB

The Spice Rack

We know that in everything God works for the good of those who love him. They are the people he called, because that was his plan.

ROMANS 8:28 NCV

Anyone who does any amount of cooking has a spice rack: that one place where all seasonings are kept within easy reach of the stovetop. There are some spices that get used consistently like garlic, salt, and pepper. And there are other spices that may only be used once in a while like cardamom, tarragon, or anise. While those lesser-used spices may collect dust in the back of our spice cupboards, we still rely on them to bring out just the right flavor in that one particular meal.

Life is a lot like a spice rack. We shelve our experiences like spices: some make so much sense—like salt and pepper—we pull from them often, clearly recognizing their usefulness. Other experiences are more subtle and undeclared. Sometimes we go years never understanding why we had them.

Then, in one moment, our life recipe will call for a little saffron. And all at once, it will make so much sense. That experience we had—the one we thought we must've had by mistake—will be the only one that matters for that moment.

Is there a season in your life that you often wonder about? You might look at that time and only see failure or waste. When you can't make sense of why it happened, remember that God will work it all for his good because you love him.

God, if I haven't seen your goodness already, I trust your Word that says good indeed will come from hardship because I love you.

We know that in everything, God works for the good of those who love him. They are the people he called, because that was his plan.

Romans 8:28 NCV

Sustained

I lay down and slept;
I awoke, for the LORD sustains me.

PSALM 3:5 NASB

There is always something to worry about, isn't there? Whether health, finances, relationships, or details, there are many unknowns in life that can easily keep us worrying.

But what if we stopped worrying? What if we stopped questioning and decided instead to feel peace? What if we could trust completely that God would take care of us and our loved ones? God is our rock, and he alone will sustain us.

The words in Psalm 3 can bring us comfort and peace when we are fearful. It speaks volumes about the grace of God: the protection and safety of his hand. But the verse goes beyond peace and comfort to the power of God. We only wake up because of his sustaining power. When we trust and believe in this God who possesses the power of life and death, what do we have to fear? Our entire lives are in his hands. We can't change that fact, so we might as well rest in it.

There will be many unknowns in your life. There will be moments when the rug feels as though it's been pulled out from under you, and there is nothing to do but wonder. In those moments that you can't control, you can trust. What are you worried about right now?

God, I take my worry right now and place it in your hands. I rest my soul, my mind, and my body in you. You alone have the power to sustain me.

I lay down and slept; I awoke, for the Lord sustains me.

Psalm 3:5 NASB

Stumbling in the Dark

The Word gave life to everything that was created,
and his life brought light to everyone.
The light shines in the darkness,
and the darkness can never extinguish it.

JOHN 1:4-5 NLT

Have you ever walked somewhere in the pitch black? You bump into things, knock stuff over, and often can't even place where you are or where you're going. Everything becomes muddled in the darkness. Without light to guide us, we can't see where we're going, or what we're running into.

Many times throughout the Bible, God likens being in sin to being in darkness. When we immerse ourselves in sin, thus rejecting the light of the truth, we can no longer see what we are running into.

Darkness will cloud our thinking and our rationale, and we won't even be able to determine what sins are coming our way. By allowing sinful messages to enter our souls through different avenues, we lose our ability to navigate our lives.

When wickedness begins to overtake your life, you lose the ability to recognize what is making you sin. Strive to keep your soul sensitive to the truth. Keep sight of the light by spending time in God's Word.

Father, I don't want to stumble around in the dark. I don't need to. Your light is bright, and pure, and forever. Help me prioritize spending time with you so I can stay close to you in the light.

The Word gave life to everything that was created.

John 1:4 NLT

Heart Center

If then you have been raised with Christ, seek the things that are above, where Christ is, seated at the right hand of God. Set your minds on things that are above, not on things that are on earth.

COLOSSIANS 3:1-2 ESV

Social media. It's an escape, a gift, a communicative tool, a joy stealer, a comparison thief, a comedian, entertainment. Social media can be fun! But it can also become an idol when we don't recognize it as such.

Suddenly, instead of opening up our Bible, we are clicking on our phones checking likes and posting photos and status updates to seek attention and approval from people rather than our Creator.

God's desire for our life is that we choose him above all else. He wants to be our focal point, one we return to time and again, so we don't ever steer too far off course. Instead of seeking approval from others, let's turn our eyes toward the one who loves us most, whose voice is the only one we should hear.

Where do you choose to spend the majority of your time? What choices could you eliminate to stay centered on Jesus? In a busy life of choices, it's important to know your back-up is also your best option: seeking God and choosing life with him.

Although communicating with people is necessary and fun, what I need more is you, God. Before I seek approval from others, I want to share my heart with you and hear what you have to say.

The Voice of Love

"The Father gives me the people who are mine.
Every one of them will come to me,
and I will always accept them."

JOHN 6:37 NCV

When we live for other voices, we will quickly become worn out and discouraged. Other people's expectations for how we should live, act, and be are sometimes unreachable.

There is one voice that matters, and it can come in a variety of forms—the voice of God.

What God would tell us is that we are loved, we are cherished, and we have significant value. We are his beloved, his children, his beautiful creation. This is the voice that matters. This is the voice to come back to when we feel like we're not enough.

What are the voices you typically listen to? Can you ignore them and focus only on the voice that matters? He will encourage you and remind you that you are enough. Nothing you do or don't do is going to make him love you any more or any less. Soak it in, so you can drown out all the other voices.

Father, I want your voice to be the loudest voice in my head. I want to be guided by you. I know you love me just as I am. You say that I am enough because you have made me enough through the work of the cross. Thank you.

Break Every Chain

He did this so that they might seek God, and perhaps they might reach out and find him, though he is not far from each one of us.

ACTS 17:27 CSB

There is a chance to start over—every day if we need to. From the inside out, we can be transformed and our hearts renewed. We can essentially remake ourselves with the help, healing, and transformative nature of Christ! Jesus died on the cross to promise us a life free from the bondage of sin, hopelessness, and any chains that try to trap us.

It can be hard to understand the complete grace offered at Calvary because we are incapable of giving that kind of grace. But when God says that he has forgotten our sin, and that he has made us new, he really means it. God is love, and love keeps no record of wrongs. Nothing can keep us from his love. Salvation tore the veil that separated us from the holiness of God. That complete work cannot be diminished or erased by anything we do.

We need to hear the truth of Christ's promise for us and stop the cycle of hopelessness, defeat, and bondage to sin. All we need to do is get on our knees and pray.

Is there an area of your life that you need to receive freedom from? Wait for God's voice to permeate the deepest, saddest parts of you. He wants you to let him take care of you. He is pursuing your heart.

God, I know that I can only find freedom in you. Thank you for loving me enough to set me free and help me with every struggle.

Glorious

I will speak of your splendor and glorious majesty
and your wondrous works.

Psalm 145:5 csb

Leaves changing from green to orange to red. Gently falling snow. A rainbow-colored sunrise. A sprout of newness in the dirt. The smell of freshly cut grass. The rustling of leaves in the trees. The smell of a pine tree at Christmas time. Billowy, moving clouds. Sunshine kissing your cheeks. It is amazing that our Creator would make all of this for us to enjoy. It's glorious, really.

Yet, days can go by, and we haven't stopped to notice. We forget to slow down. We ignore this incredibly beautiful world that he made for us to explore and enjoy. It is amazing what a walk with a friend, a run through the woods, or the feel of bare feet on grass can do for the soul.

Do you take time to get outside and enjoy all that God created?

The next time you're feeling a bit squirmy, slow down, take a walk outside, and soak in his presence that's all around you: in the grass between your toes, in the rustle of leaves in front of you, and in the sunshine kissing your cheeks.

God, you have made everything so beautiful. Thank you for the joys in simple life, for the beauty in every tiny detail of your creation. When I take time to stop and ponder your works, I am awestruck. You are amazing.

I will
speak of your
splendor and
glorious
majesty and
your wondrous
works.

Psalm 145:5 CSB

God's Ear

I love the LORD, for he heard my voice;
he heard my cry for mercy.
Because he turned his ear to me,
I will call on him as long as I live.

PSALM 116:1-2 NIV

God hears you. Whether you are shouting praises of thanksgiving, crying tears of mourning, or singing phrases of glory, God hears. He listens. He does not abandon or ignore you.

He hears your voice. He hears your heart. He hears your shouts, your whispers, and your thoughts. Sometimes this seems scary; we feel like we have to perform. That is a lie. Do not believe it. God takes us as we are, where we are. We don't have to filter, pretend, or please. He meets us, loves us, and accepts us just as we are in this moment.

Do you believe God hears you? What do you want to tell him right now? He is a beautiful, caring God who takes us as sinners and holds our hand as we walk the path to salvation.

Father God, thank you for listening to me in all my different emotions. You are full of compassion, and you have been so good to me. I am blessed to be called your child.

Rest in Jesus

He who dwells in the secret place of the Most High
Shall abide under the shadow of the Almighty.

Psalm 91:1 NKJV

Have you ever been awake when you think no one else is? Maybe you had an early morning flight, and you feel you are the only person who could possibly be stirring at that hour. It feels kind of magical, doesn't it? It's like you have an unshared secret.

Regardless of you being a night owl, morning person, or somewhere in-between, there is peace that comes with meeting Jesus in secret, when your world has stopped for a bit.

Whatever it looks like, rising early or staying up late, taking a work break, a study break, or a mommy break, finding that quiet is where you can actually acquire strength. We need spiritual food to conquer each day.

Can you find daily quiet time to meet with Jesus? He will meet you in that space, filling you with peace, strength, and love to go out and conquer the world.

Meeting with you in my secret place is so refreshing, Lord. You fill my heart with hope and give me everything I need to get through each day. Thank you that I can find rest in you.

Change of Season

"Be strong and courageous, and act; do not fear nor be dismayed, for the LORD God, my God, is with you. He will not fail you nor forsake you until all the work for the service of the house of the LORD is finished."

1 Chronicles 28:20 nasb

The change of seasons can bring a variety of feelings. Hope, anxiety, excitement, expectation, or worry can knock at your door each time the weather changes. Just as the physical season shifts are natural and needed, spiritual and emotional seasons are necessary as well.

You will experience various seasons in your life: seasons of longing and contentment, seasons of discouragement and joy, seasons of more and less.

Seasons can be challenging. They require bravery, obedience, dedication, and sometimes total upheaval of everything comfortable. If we feel that impending corner of a season change, it usually means God is preparing us for something different—a change. In those seasons of life, the one who won't change, won't back down, and won't leave us stranded is our heavenly Father.

Do you see an impending season change approaching? Be brave! God will not move you into something without giving you the grace to make it through.

Just like with natural seasons, God, there are some spiritual seasons I like better than others. Winter is hard. Spring is hopeful. But I know you have blessings and intentions for each season of life I'm in. Help me see your purposes and rejoice in them.

Joyous Journey

Consider it pure joy, my brothers and sisters, whenever you face trials of many kinds, because you know that the testing of your faith produces perseverance. Let perseverance finish its work so that you may be mature and complete, not lacking anything.

JAMES 1:2-4 NIV

There is great joy in the journey: in the mundane details, in the difficult times, in the confusing moments, and in the tears. There is so much joy to be found in the quiet and in the noise.

Pity parties and comparisons create a direct path for the enemy to steal our joy. There is hope in Jesus and the gift of little joy-filled moments. They come in varying forms: sunshine rays pouring in the windows, a nice person at the check-out counter, a turn-the-radio-as-high-as-it-can-go kind of song, a dance party in the living room, or the taste of a delicious meal after a long day.

Whatever the moment, there is joy if we look for it.

There's a journey of joy in waking up every day knowing it's another day to breathe in the fresh air, head to dinner with a friend, or grab coffee with a co-worker. Find joy in the moment.

God, there really is joy to be found in every moment I am alive. You have blessed me with breath, friendship, and opportunity. Thank you for each new day and all the joy there is to be found in it.

He Knows

The Spirit helps us with our weakness. We do not know how to pray as we should. But the Spirit himself speaks to God for us, even begs God for us with deep feelings that words cannot explain.

ROMANS 8:26 NCV

You stare at the menu overwhelmed by choices. Pasta sounds yummy, but you're avoiding carbs. Salad sounds healthy, but you just had that for lunch. Steak sounds perfect until you look at the price. Everyone else has ordered: all eyes are on you. You know you're hungry; you just don't know what for.

"What do I want?" you ask, though not expecting an answer.

There are days prayer can feel like that. We know we want something—we sense an ache or longing—but can't quite identify it. Other times, we're simply in too much pain to focus. We need, we need... but we can't get the words out.

"What do I want?" we cry. This time, we can expect an answer. The Holy Spirit, because he lives inside us, knows us so intimately he can actually step in and pray on our behalf. He knows even when we don't.

Spend some time with the Spirit today. Thank him for knowing your heart and sharing it with God when you can't.

God, I don't always have words for what is going on in my heart. I can come up with plenty of catch phrases and clichés, but those are meaningless at times. Thank you that you hear my heart, and you speak for me. Do that for me today as I spend time with you.

Being Known

You know what I long for, LORD;
you hear my every sigh.

PSALM 38:9 NLT

Think of the most perfect gift you've ever received. Not the most extravagant, but the one that was just so perfectly you that you realized the giver really knew you.

Your gift giver heard you that one time when you mentioned that one thing, perhaps in passing. And because they were listening with their heart, they saw into yours. They got you.

We love to be understood and long to be seen. For many of us it's how we know we are loved. How much, then, must the Father love us? He who knows everything about us—who takes the time to listen to every longing and comfort every sigh—is waiting to give us his perfect gifts. We are known. We are loved.

Share your longing with God today. Let him show you his great love by revealing how intimately he knows you. Let him give you a good and perfect gift.

I'll admit, God, some days there are a lot of sighs coming from me. Thank you that you know what each sigh means, and you know exactly what I need. Your gifts are good and perfect because you know me better than anyone else, and you love me fully.

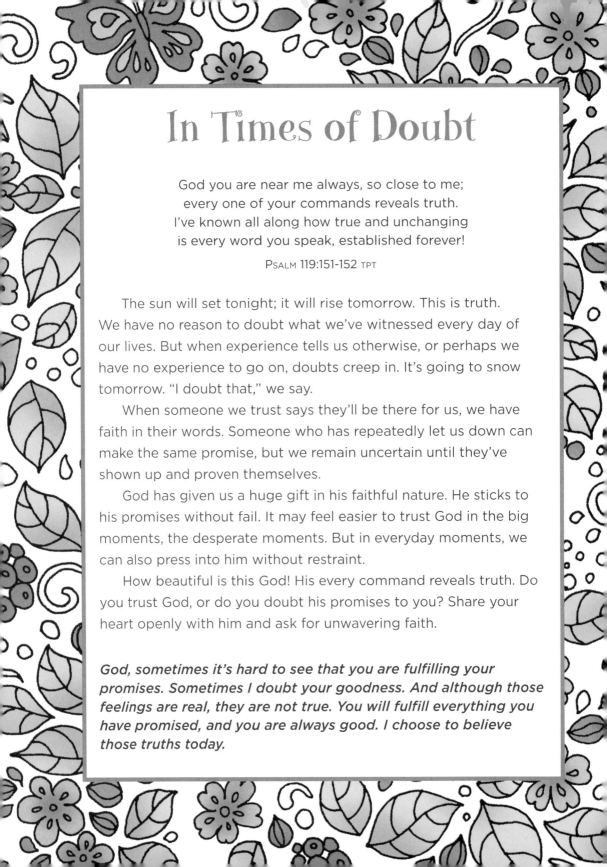

In Times of Doubt

God you are near me always, so close to me;
every one of your commands reveals truth.
I've known all along how true and unchanging
is every word you speak, established forever!

Psalm 119:151-152 TPT

The sun will set tonight; it will rise tomorrow. This is truth. We have no reason to doubt what we've witnessed every day of our lives. But when experience tells us otherwise, or perhaps we have no experience to go on, doubts creep in. It's going to snow tomorrow. "I doubt that," we say.

When someone we trust says they'll be there for us, we have faith in their words. Someone who has repeatedly let us down can make the same promise, but we remain uncertain until they've shown up and proven themselves.

God has given us a huge gift in his faithful nature. He sticks to his promises without fail. It may feel easier to trust God in the big moments, the desperate moments. But in everyday moments, we can also press into him without restraint.

How beautiful is this God! His every command reveals truth. Do you trust God, or do you doubt his promises to you? Share your heart openly with him and ask for unwavering faith.

God, sometimes it's hard to see that you are fulfilling your promises. Sometimes I doubt your goodness. And although those feelings are real, they are not true. You will fulfill everything you have promised, and you are always good. I choose to believe those truths today.

Please Remain Seated

"Remain in me, as I also remain in you. No branch
can bear fruit by itself; it must remain in the vine.
Neither can you bear fruit unless you remain in me."

JOHN 15:4 NIV

When riding in a moving car, boat, or plane, we wouldn't just jump out, no matter how restless or impatient we were feeling. That would be crazy. We couldn't possibly expect to arrive at our destination as safely or as quickly—or perhaps at all. We grasp the necessity of remaining where we are if we are to get where we are going.

Why then are we so quick to jump ahead when it comes to God's plans for our lives? We accept his grace but not his timing. We welcome his comfort but not his discipline.

How often do we decide without praying, or act without his prompting? And yet we expect to get where we are going—safely, quickly, easily.

Are there areas of your life you are trying to direct on your own? Spend some time praying for the Spirit to reveal to you anywhere you are not abiding in Jesus or trusting his timing. Ask him to help you trust him.

God, I confess my need to control my schedule and my life. I want to give this over to you and let you show me where I could abide in you better. I trust you to do what is perfect for me, and that means I have to trust your timing. Help me in this, Lord.

Trust the Light

"I am the Light of the world; he who follows Me will not walk in the darkness, but will have the Light of life."

JOHN 8:12 NASB

Imagine yourself in total darkness, perhaps a wilderness camping trip (or a power failure at a nice hotel if that's more your speed). It's the middle of the night, and you must find your way back to camp.

Turn on your flashlight. Though it only illuminates a few steps at a time, it's enough to keep moving. Each step forward lights more of the way, and eventually you see your destination.

Our faith walk is very much like this. Most of the time, we can't see where we're headed. Although just a few steps ahead is all we can make out for certain, we trust the path the light reveals.

Jesus is our light. He shows us just what we need to see to put one foot forward at a time. Ask him to help you ignore the unseen and trust the light.

God, just as I see better in the darkness with a flashlight to illuminate my path, I see better when I let you shine on my life and show me the best way to proceed. When it's hard to put one foot in front of the other, give me the grace and strength I need to continue.

Our Comforter

Praise be to the God and Father of our Lord Jesus Christ,
the Father of compassion and the God of all comfort,
who comforts us in all our troubles, so that we can comfort those
in any trouble with the comfort we ourselves receive from God.

2 Corinthians 1:3-4 niv

It's the end of a long, difficult day. All you want to do is crawl in bed, wrap up in your comforter, and rest. Something about a soft, fluffy blanket helps problems seem less like problems.

One of God's many names is the God of all comfort. He is our ultimate comforter, allowing us to wrap ourselves in him and be warmed, reassured, and relieved. He does this so we can pay it forward, wrapping ourselves around others in need of comfort and showing them his love.

Notice the repetition in the verses above. The word comfort appears four times. This isn't because Paul was feeling uninspired; it's because he wanted to make sure we heard him. We are comforted so that we can comfort. God wants both for us. Which have you done more of lately? Ask him to help you with the other.

Whether being comforted, or comforting others, God, I need your compassion. That fills me with peace for myself and peace to pour out on others. Thank you that difficult situations are never wasted. You give me opportunities to share with others in their need for comfort.

Finding Peace

You will keep in perfect peace
all who trust in you,
all whose thoughts are fixed on you!

ISAIAH 26:3 NLT

What does chaos look like in your world? Crazy work deadlines, over-scheduled activities, long to-do lists and short hours? All of the above? How about peace? What does that look like?

Most of us immediately picture having gotten away, whether to the deep soaking tub or a sunny beach. It's quiet. Serene. The trouble with that image, lovely as it is, is that it's fleeting.

We can't live in our bathtubs or in Fiji, so our best bet is to seek out peace right in the middle of our chaos. Guess what? We can have it. Jesus promises peace to all who put him first.

How appealing is it to imagine being unmoved by the stresses in your life? Is it easy or difficult for you to claim this promise for yourself? Ask Jesus to grant you true peace; fix your thoughts on him and watch the rest of the world fade away. When it tries to sneak back in, ask him again.

God, finding true peace in this crazy world is impossible. I can relax in the hot sun and warm water on a tropical island for a week, but the peace found there is still only temporary. Lasting peace only comes from keeping my mind fixed on you. That's the peace I want.

You will keep in perfect peace all who trust in you, all whose thoughts are fixed on you.

Isaiah 26:3 NLT

Where Credit Is Due

"Give praise to the LORD, proclaim his name;
make known among the nations what he has done,
and proclaim that his name is exalted.
Sing to the LORD, for he has done glorious things;
let this be known to all the world."

ISAIAH 12:4-5 NIV

You achieve a goal, or you get some wonderful news. The day you've been waiting for has arrived, and you're so excited about it. What is your first reaction? Do you update your status on social media to let your friends know what you've done? Do you call your mom and tell her the wonderful news?

There's nothing wrong with sharing your excitement with others. But when doing so, be sure to first give the glory and praise to God. He has given you everything you have. Get excited about how good he has been to you.

When you're just so happy that you can't help but dance for joy, be sure to give Jesus a twirl too. He wants to celebrate with you!

Are you giving credit where it's due? Be sure to take some time today to thank the Lord for all that he has helped you achieve and for all that he has given you. He wants to share in your excitement!

Thank you, God, for everything that you have helped me to accomplish. You have done many great things in and through my life, and you deserve all the glory for them.

Weary to the Core

The steps of the God-pursuing ones
follow firmly in the footsteps of the Lord.
And God delights in every step they take to follow him.
If they stumble badly they will still survive,
for the Lord lifts them up with his hands.

PSALM 37:23-24 TPT

Have you ever been run so ragged that you just didn't know if you could take even one more step? Your calendar is a blur of scheduled activities, your days are full, your every hour is blocked off for this or that, and it's hard to find even a spare minute for yourself. Even your very bones feel weary, and you fall into your bed at night, drained from it all.

There is someone who is ready to catch you when you fall. You might stumble throughout your busy day, but he will never let you hit the floor as you take a tumble.

God delights in you! He will direct your every step if you ask him to. He will gladly take you by the hand and guide you.

Are you allowing the Lord to guide your days? Though you may be weary, he has enough energy to get you through it all. Hold out your hand to him today and walk side-by-side with Jesus.

Never-ending energy sounds incredible, God. And you have it! Help me to draw from you each day, so I have the energy needed to live my life in a way that brings you honor and glory. You can sustain me in my weakest moments.

Losing to Gain

"If you try to hang on to your life, you will lose it.
But if you give up your life for my sake, you will save it."

Matthew 16:25 NLT

The key to growing in your faith is simple. There must be less of us in order to have more of God. To allow more of his presence into our lives, we must give up more of ourselves. We need to place our lives before him as an offering and give him our all.

The world would say that giving up ourselves is a loss. We've been taught for years that we must put ourselves first. Our fellow man would say that we need to make ourselves a priority. But oh, are they missing out!

When we give ourselves over completely to God, we get to share in his glory and in his great joy. Setting aside our earthly pleasures for heavenly treasures means we gain a lot more than what this world could ever offer us.

What desires do you find yourself holding onto? Empty yourself of the desires of your flesh and allow God to fill you with his presence. You won't feel a lack. In fact, it will overflow in your life, spilling out everywhere for others to see!

God, losing my life sounds scary. All around me, the world says I should make decisions that benefit me, that I should do everything I can to better my position in life. The reality is that I can only truly find my life by giving it to you. Help me to keep this perspective at the front of my mind.

If you
give up
your life
for my sake,
you will
save it.

Matthew 16:25 NLT

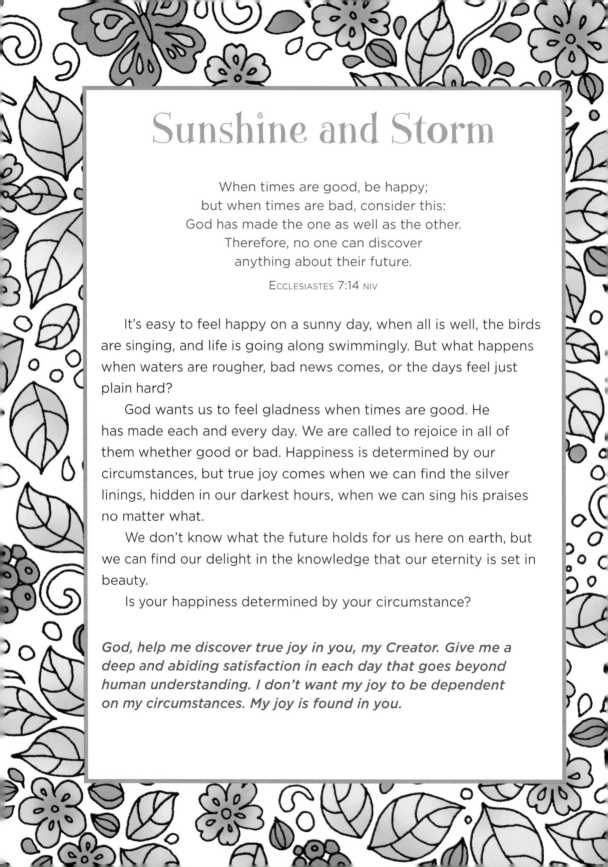

Sunshine and Storm

When times are good, be happy;
but when times are bad, consider this:
God has made the one as well as the other.
Therefore, no one can discover
anything about their future.

ECCLESIASTES 7:14 NIV

It's easy to feel happy on a sunny day, when all is well, the birds are singing, and life is going along swimmingly. But what happens when waters are rougher, bad news comes, or the days feel just plain hard?

God wants us to feel gladness when times are good. He has made each and every day. We are called to rejoice in all of them whether good or bad. Happiness is determined by our circumstances, but true joy comes when we can find the silver linings, hidden in our darkest hours, when we can sing his praises no matter what.

We don't know what the future holds for us here on earth, but we can find our delight in the knowledge that our eternity is set in beauty.

Is your happiness determined by your circumstance?

God, help me discover true joy in you, my Creator. Give me a deep and abiding satisfaction in each day that goes beyond human understanding. I don't want my joy to be dependent on my circumstances. My joy is found in you.

We Have Time

Be careful how you live. Don't live like fools, but like those who are wise. Make the most of every opportunity in these evil days. Don't act thoughtlessly, but understand what the Lord wants you to do.

EPHESIANS 5:15-17 NLT

Time is one of those things we never seem to have enough of. Many of our days can feel like a race against the clock to get everything done. We seem to lack the time we need for even the most important things—things like being in God's Word, spending intentional time with loved ones, or volunteering to help those in need.

At the end of the day, there is one reality we must remember: we have time for what we make time for.

It's easy to feel busy, but what are we truly busying ourselves with? Are we finding time to spend browsing social media or watching re-runs of our favorite TV shows? Are we finding time to take a long shower or sleep for a few extra minutes in the morning? None of those things are necessarily wrong, but if we feel pressed for time and are unable to spend time with the Lord, we may need to rethink where our time goes.

Take a good hard look at your day today. How can you spend your time wisely, in a way that will make the most of the moments and opportunities you have.

God, help me to be wise with my choices today. I want to make the most of the opportunities you have put before me. Show me where to put my efforts so they are blessed.

A Thankful Heart

Whatever you do, whether in word or deed, do it all in the name of
the Lord Jesus, giving thanks to God the Father through him.

COLOSSIANS 3:17 NIV

Have you ever noticed on vacation that your heart feels lighter?
That you worry less and are more thankful? Cultivating a heart of
thankfulness can shift our entire perspective on life.

When we are grateful, we start to see the light of God so much
more. We start to see him everywhere.

A thankful heart is a heart that refuses to let the enemy in and
deceive us. Suddenly our circumstances seem not so terrible, our
problems not so huge. A heart of gratitude glorifies God and keeps
us centered on him. Just like on vacation, you can have that same
perspective every day even in the most mundane circumstances.

What can you do to start cultivating a heart of gratitude? A
heart of thankfulness keeps you grounded in Christ, in communion
with him, and allows you to live the fullest life he's designed for you.

*I am thankful for all of the blessings you have placed in my life,
God. You have surrounded me with goodness; I see that better
when I have a heart of thankfulness. Let that be my default—
gratitude!*

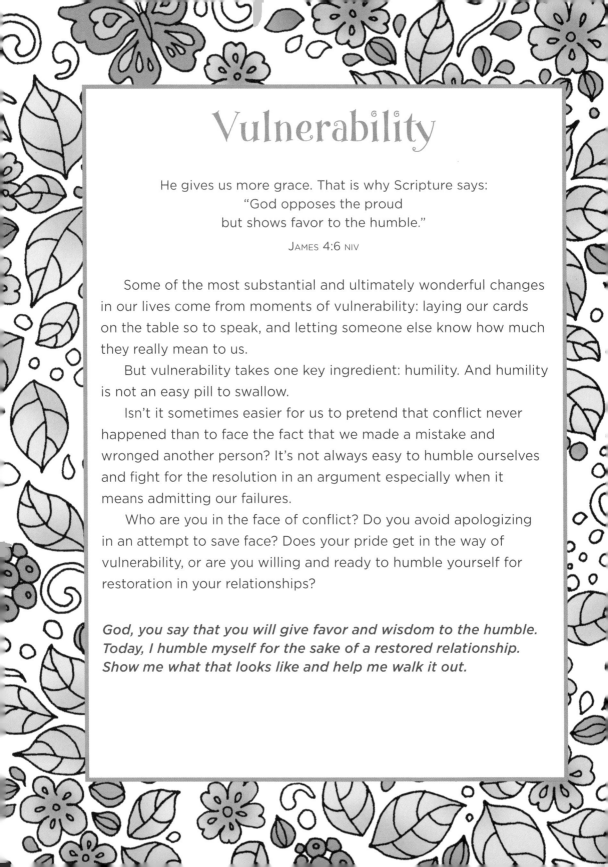

Vulnerability

He gives us more grace. That is why Scripture says:
"God opposes the proud
but shows favor to the humble."

JAMES 4:6 NIV

Some of the most substantial and ultimately wonderful changes in our lives come from moments of vulnerability: laying our cards on the table so to speak, and letting someone else know how much they really mean to us.

But vulnerability takes one key ingredient: humility. And humility is not an easy pill to swallow.

Isn't it sometimes easier for us to pretend that conflict never happened than to face the fact that we made a mistake and wronged another person? It's not always easy to humble ourselves and fight for the resolution in an argument especially when it means admitting our failures.

Who are you in the face of conflict? Do you avoid apologizing in an attempt to save face? Does your pride get in the way of vulnerability, or are you willing and ready to humble yourself for restoration in your relationships?

God, you say that you will give favor and wisdom to the humble. Today, I humble myself for the sake of a restored relationship. Show me what that looks like and help me walk it out.

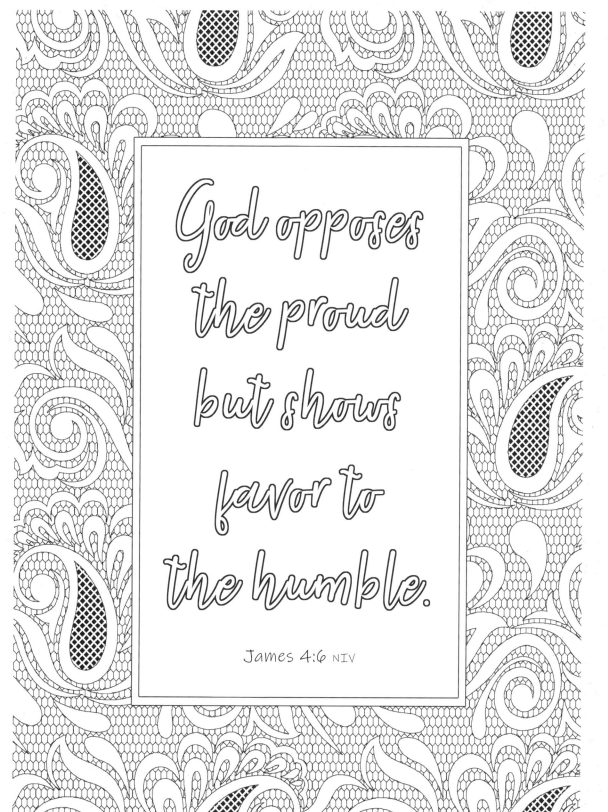

God opposes the proud but shows favor to the humble.

James 4:6 NIV

River of Peace

"I am the LORD your God,
who teaches you what is best for you,
who directs you in the way you should go.
Your peace would have been like a river,
your well-being like the waves of the sea."

Isaiah 48:17-18 NIV

Where do you usually go to find peace? Is there a certain place? A certain person?

One of the greatest gifts of God is his undeniable, unfathomable peace. It is a deep well that comes with knowing and experiencing Jesus' love. No matter where we are, where we are going, and whatever we might be experiencing, his peace is greater.

Grasp how deep his well runs. Lasting peace and joy does not come in the world or in people around you. Although those can be comforting, true, transforming, and powerful, peace can only come from our Father. And oh, how he loves when we come to his well.

Where do you usually turn for peace? Have you experienced the indescribable peace of God?

When I walk in your way, Father, you lead me into what is best for me. You know that better than I do. Help me to understand the benefit of living in your will and surrendering my own. You are my peace.

Thirst for Pure Water

I want more than anything
to be in the courtyards of the LORD's Temple.
My whole being wants
to be with the living God.

PSALM 84:2 NCV

Have you ever noticed that the more consistently you drink water, the more your body thirsts for it? And the less you drink water, the less you consciously desire it. Though you still need water to live, you become satisfied with small amounts of it disguised in other foods and drinks.

For a body that has become accustomed to pure water on a daily basis, only straight water will quench its thirst.

The same principle applies to God's presence in our lives. The more we enter his presence, the more we long to stay there. The more we sit at his feet and listen to what he has to say, the more we need his Word to continue living. But if we allow ourselves to become satisfied with candy-coated truth and secondhand revelation, we will slowly begin to lose our hunger for the pure, untainted presence of the living God.

Does your entire being long to be with God? Press into Jesus until you can no longer be satisfied with anything less than the purest form of his presence. Cultivate your hunger and your fascination with him until you crave him.

God, I want to spend my life feasting on your truth, knowing your character, and adoring your heart. Help me desire you—the purest form of water.

No Condemnation

Straightening up, Jesus said to her, "Woman, where are they? Did no one condemn you?" She said, "No one, Lord." And Jesus said, "I do not condemn you, either. Go. From now on do not sin any longer."

JOHN 8:10-11 NASB

Most of us know the story of the woman caught in adultery. One of the intriguing moments was when Jesus was questioned about whether or not the adulteress should be stoned. Jesus' response was to stoop down and start writing in the dirt.

Though we don't know exactly what Jesus wrote that day, the action of stooping down defined one interpretation of the word *grace*.

As everyone else stood casting judgment, Jesus removed himself from the accusers, stooping low and occupying himself elsewhere. It spoke volumes about his lack of participation in the crowd's judgment.

Because of Jesus' distraction, the eyes of the onlookers were drawn off the woman, perhaps lifting a portion of her shame. With their attention focused on Jesus, he said the words that saved the woman's life: "Let him who has never sinned cast the first stone." One by one, the accusers walked away. Jesus was the only one qualified to throw a stone; he chose grace instead. And he does the same for you.

God, you are merciful and forgiving. Thank you for lifting my sin and shame and offering me forgiveness and hope. You do not condemn me or remind me of my sin. You forgive completely and draw me closer. I am so grateful to be called your child.

Growth

I do not mean that I am already as God wants me to be. I have not yet reached that goal, but I continue trying to reach it and to make it mine. Christ wants me to do that, which is the reason he made me his.

PHILIPPIANS 3:12 NCV

Do you remember when you realized you had stopped growing? Your height was going to be your height, your shoe size your shoe size. This second fact was pretty thrilling for many of us; no more hearing Mom say, "That's too much to spend on shoes you'll outgrow in a few months." And so the collection began.

Not too long after our bones finish growing, we realize the real growth is just getting started. As we become young women, friendships either deepen or fade away as we begin to figure out who we are.

No matter what your age is today, you are likely still working on different areas in your life. When you are growing in Christ, it's a process that never really ends. You don't wake up one day and say, "I have arrived." The older you get, the more you realize how much you have to learn and grow.

How does knowing that God wants to help you become your best inspire you to attempt it?

Father God, help me as I continue to grow in all different areas of my life. Give me a teachable spirit that causes a desire to be my very best. I want to grow under your guidance and care.

A Shining Example

We are God's handiwork, created in Christ Jesus to do good works,
which God prepared in advance for us to do.

Ephesians 2:10 niv

When we accept the gift of Christ's salvation, we can be assured that we will live for eternity with our Father in heaven. There is nothing that we can do by our actions alone that ensures a place for us. But that doesn't mean the buck stops there. Though not a requirement for admittance through the pearly gates, a life lived doing good deeds is something every Christ follower should seek to attain.

As Christians, we are an extension of the Lord during our time on earth. God has given you the grace for today to be an example of his light and love; you don't have to try to be anybody else. Just be the way he created you to be!

You may not have thought today was much different from the last, and perhaps you don't see the good deeds that you have done as being particularly spiritual. Remember that God created you as an image-bearer, and just by choosing to following Jesus you are being like Jesus.

Be encouraged that you are a shining example of his love, and others will see how a life with Christ is a beautiful one.

Thank you, Jesus, for showing me how to live a life of love and humility. Help others to see my good works and to recognize that my life has been marked by you.

Constant Complaint

Do all things without complaining or arguments; so that you will prove yourselves to be blameless and innocent, children of God above reproach in the midst of a crooked and perverse generation, among whom you appear as lights in the world, holding firmly the word of life, so that on the day of Christ I can take pride because I did not run in vain nor labor in vain.

PHILIPPIANS 2:14-16 NASB

The temptation to complain or bicker can be overwhelming at times. Get a group of women together in a room and you can almost see the tension grow. "She did this and it wasn't fair." "He doesn't contribute the way he should." "My life is hard for a multitude of reasons." The list goes on and on.

Our complaints are often valid and true, but we miss the joy that God desires for us when we seek out only the negative. Choose to be positive and truthful today!

Choosing to be positive and to speak positively is something that will make you stand out like the stars against a black sky.

This letter from Paul to the Philippians was written thousands of years ago, but it could just have easily been written today. We still live in a warped and crooked generation. Let's shine like stars in the sky! Let us hold firmly to his Word as we speak life to those around us.

God, I often get pulled into the negativity of this world, so I ask that I would be sensitive to the prompting of the Holy Spirit when I start to head down that path. Keep my words full of life and love.

Keeping a Secret

A gossip goes around revealing a secret,
but a trustworthy person keeps a confidence.

<small>PROVERBS 11:13 CSB</small>

We've all been there before. A friend leans in and whispers, "Did you hear about what she did?" And something in us wants to know. To hear the scoop. To spread the word. It's almost as if we are built to be mean. To share what we know of others' downfalls and fallacies.

It might feel good in the moment to tear people down because then we are not alone in the many ways we fall short. But we were designed to lift one another up. We should strive to be worthy of knowing a friend's secrets because we will keep the knowledge to ourselves.

Have you been more aware of gossip today? It's an easy trap to fall into but be encouraged to continue to allow the Holy Spirit to shape your response to gossip.

The next time you are tempted to share what isn't yours to tell, take a deep breath and pause. Ask yourself if betraying a confidence is worth letting down a friend. Allow yourself to be the type of friend that God has designed you to be.

Jesus, you are my best friend. Thank you that I can confidently confide in you. Help me to be that kind of friend to others. If people confide in me today, help me to be a true and trustworthy friend.

Childish Behavior

Whoever keeps His word, truly the love of God is perfected in him.
By this we know that we are in Him. He who says he abides
in Him ought himself also to walk just as He walked.

1 John 2:5-6 NKJV

It can be difficult to obey God. Even as grown women, everything in us sometimes wants to stomp and shout, "No!" When life throws hard tasks our way, we want to flee. We want to submit to our own desires and ignore what God is asking of us.

When the child in you threatens to rise up and make choices for you, stop and pray. Lean in closer to the Lord and ask him for his help in choosing obedience. It's only with his guidance that we are able to be made complete and leave the foot stomping to the little ones.

Scripture says that obedience will make us whole in our relationship with God. We will truly know what love means when we choose obedience. We cannot claim to know him and love him if we are not living by his Word.

When we live in God, as Jesus did, we are surrendering our hearts to him. We are allowing an open and truthful communication with our heavenly Father. Jesus spoke of living in the Father, and the Father living in him. You are invited to join this intimate union.

Heavenly Father, you are such a wonderful God. Guide me into your truth today, so I know what is right and what is wrong. Give me understanding of what it means to live in you.

whoever keeps
His word, truly the
love of God is
perfected in him.

1 John 2:5 NKJV

Checklist

"You will seek me and find me when you
seek me with all your heart."

Jeremiah 29:13 niv

It's easy to go about our day crossing our many to-do items off our lists and making sure we accomplish all our tasks. Sometimes spending time with the Lord can become just another box to check off. Toilets? Cleaned. Groceries? Purchased. Scripture reading? Check.

Are you holding back in your relationship with God, or have you given him all your heart? Don't reserve anything. Give all of yourself to him! Seek him in all areas of your life. He is there wherever you look, waiting for you, wanting to connect with you.

The Lord wants so much more out of his relationship with us than to be merely another chore to accomplish or another bullet point on our checklist. He is more than a small portion of your day, forgotten after you've closed your Bible. Search for him; he wants to be found! He wants to show you all that can be had when you desire true relationship with him.

You might not have had time in your day to pause and think about your relationship with God, but you can change that right now. Be still and allow him to speak to you now.

Lord, I desire a real relationship with you. Let me seek you with all my heart so I can find you. Thank you that you are always near. I take these quiet moments to reflect on my relationship with you. I want to pursue what you want for my life. Speak to me.

You will
seek me
and find me
when you
seek me
with all
your heart.

Jeremiah 29:13 NIV

Losing to Win

He summoned the crowd together with His disciples, and said to them, "If anyone wants to come after Me, he must deny himself, take up his cross, and follow Me. For whoever wans to save his life will lose it, but whoever loses his life for My sake and the gospel's will save it."

MARK 8:34-35 NASB

Selfish. The word itself is an ugly one. It brings to mind all that is unflattering. There is no denying that we want, first and foremost, what's best for us in life. But what is best for others?

Take a close look at your life. In what areas have you become wrapped up in yourself? Give those areas to the Lord and seek his will for your life.

It can be easy to get caught up in the day and think only about your needs and wants. It is just as easy to put your emotions ahead of acting the right way toward someone.

Scripture plainly says that we are not to put ourselves first. If we try to hang on to our selfish ways, we will lose our lives. But we are saved when we take up our cross and follow Christ instead. When we say no to the flesh, we say yes to so much more.

Lord, I'm sorry when I have been consumed with thinking about all the things that I want in life. Help me to be aware of the needs of others around me and to imitate you by laying aside my desires for the sake of others.

Born for Relationship

The LORD God said, "It is not good that man should be alone;
I will make him a helper comparable to him."

GENESIS 2:18 NKJV

Before the human race ever came into existence, there was relationship. The Father, Son, and Holy Spirit co-existed in a loving bond with one another. They were interdependent, in need of connection with others. They were the very first example of what it means to feel kinship.

If you feel lonely, take stock how you may have put up walls to prevent true friendship from happening. Are you getting in your own way of developing strong bonds with others? Pray that the Lord will place people in your life who will be a source of authentic relationship. Seek ways to mature these connections beginning today!

Because we were created in God's image, we were made for relationship with each other. We crave it. Scripture tells us that it isn't good for us to be alone, so why is it that we often feel so lonely? We can be standing in a room full of people and feel no connection with any one of them.

Are there moments you can reflect on when you could have connected on a deeper level with others but didn't? Ask God to give you wisdom to know who you can trust.

Lord God, you don't want me to be alone. Please help me to be open and vulnerable so I can begin to form deeper connections.

It is not good that man should be alone; I will make him a helper comparable to him.

Genesis 2:18 NKJV

Mountain Movers

Without faith it is impossible to please God, since the one
who draws near to him must believe that he exists
and that he rewards those who seek him.

HEBREWS 11:6 CSB

Jesus said that if we have faith as small as a mustard seed,
we can move mountains. Since none of us have plans to pick up
Mount Kilimanjaro and find a new spot for it, how can we apply this
knowledge to our lives? Truly, it sounds a bit wacky that we can do
great things with only a little faith. And yet, Scripture tells us that
it's so!

How can you step out in faith? It looks different for everyone.
For some, the first step may be giving themselves fully to a belief
that Christ died for their sins. For others, it could look like jumping
out of a job that isn't a good fit and taking a leap into the unknown,
or giving up a toxic relationship knowing that the Lord will be there
to take care of them.

Seek God's will for your life today. How does he want you to
take a leap? What does that look like? Spend some time reflecting
on this today; he wants to reward you for your faith!

When you believe that God truly exists and you decide to seek
him with all your heart, your faith will build, and you will be able to
ask him boldly for the rewards of life.

*Lord, show me where I need to have more faith. Help me to trust
in you so I can earnestly seek you for answers and do amazing
things for you. Build my faith today.*

Under His Wing

He will cover you with his feathers.
He will shelter you with his wings.
His faithful promises are your armor and protection.

Psalm 91:4 NLT

At some point, each of us feels hurt. We feel pain that goes beyond what we think we can bear, that pushes us to the brink of what we think we can handle, that leaves us bruised and brokenhearted. And we feel so alone in our grief.

Give your pain to God. Cry out to him. He wants to give you peace. Let him take you under his wing and shelter you from all that hurts you. Show him your wounds and allow him to heal them today. Rest in the knowledge that you are never alone.

There is someone who is always with you, ready to comfort you. Jesus doesn't want you to live in pain. He wants to give you refuge.

You may not know why you are bearing your particular burden. It often feels unfair, but you need to know that you can go to God in the middle of your pain and find relief.

Lord, thank you for your presence with me even now. Give me a moment of peace from my hurt and pain. Wrap me in your arms and allow me to experience your comfort. I pray for others who are hurting and ask for your peace in their life.

He will cover you
with his feathers.
He will shelter you
with his wings.
His faithful promises
are your armor
and protection.

Psalm 91:4 NLT

Tossed by Wind

When you ask, you must believe and not doubt,
because the one who doubts is like a wave of the sea,
blown and tossed by the wind.

JAMES 1:6 NIV

There's nothing quite like the feeling of riding on a boat on a beautiful day. It can be incredibly relaxing, leaning back and enjoying the gentle rocking of the waves. But have you ever been out on the water during a storm? It's anything but relaxing. In fact, being tossed around by dangerous winds as the waves grow larger is downright scary.

Sometimes it might feel like life is tossing you around. Remember that it is not your circumstances that determine your anxiety; it is your faith. Pray for wisdom! And when you do, make sure you are ready to receive it. Believe the word God has for you, and do not doubt.

When James paints a picture of what happens when we doubt, it should be taken seriously. After all, his generation definitely knew what it was like to be at sea. They depended on fishing for much of what they ate! And with none of today's technology and gear to save them from a storm, the danger was very real.

It's important to have faith, and it is hard not to doubt. But if you ask God for just that, he will happily give it to you.

Lord, forgive my unbelief! It is hard to believe that things will get easier or more calm, but I pray that as I rest in you, you will bring faith and peace into my thoughts. I ask, believing in your goodness and faithfulness to me.

Hand Over Control

They won't be afraid of bad news;
their hearts are steady because they trust in the LORD.
They are confident and will not be afraid;
they will look down on their enemies.

PSALM 112:7-8 NCV

The phone rings, and with it, your heart sinks. It's the bad news you've been dreading. The news that could make you question everything you know. Suddenly, you're in the middle of a struggle. Why would the Lord allow such terrible things to happen if he truly loved you?

Trust is a tricky thing. When you fully trust someone, you completely give yourself over to them. And when you fully trust God, you allow him to take the reins of your life; you give him all the control.

You're no longer in the driver's seat—you're an active passenger, riding shotgun. And though it's difficult, giving of yourself completely means that you don't have to fear the bad that may come. God has it in his very capable hands.

Have you given control of your life to God, or are you the passenger who can't help but give directions during the ride? Release your worries and cares to him and allow him to carry your burden for you. He is strong enough to handle it.

Lord, I want you to be in control. In the various trials of life, I need to know that I am not alone and that I can be secure in your help. Give me the strength I need today.

True Worship

God is Spirit, so those who worship him
must worship in spirit and in truth."

JOHN 4:24 NLT

When was the last time you gave yourself over fully to a time of worship? Not just singing along to the words in church, not just bowing your head in prayer, but letting yourself be completely consumed by the presence of God? That is the kind of worship the Father seeks!

Take some quiet time today to allow his mighty presence to wash over you. Revel in the time you have with him, worshiping him in whatever way feels natural to you. You'll discover that he is indeed worthy of your adoring reverence.

True worship is quite different than just singing along. We serve a God who is awesome and powerful. He is deserving of our utmost devotion. When we discover just how amazing he is, we know that he is worth our full praise.

People can talk about worshipping God and show all kinds of outward devotion like lengthy prayers, splayed hands in the air, or intense biblical debate. But God is after the heart; that's what he really wants from us.

Lord, I know that sometimes I compare myself to other people who seem to be more spiritual than I am. Thank you for confronting me with the truth: that it isn't about the songs I sing or the way I show my worship. You care about a heart that is directed to you. I give you my heart's attention now.

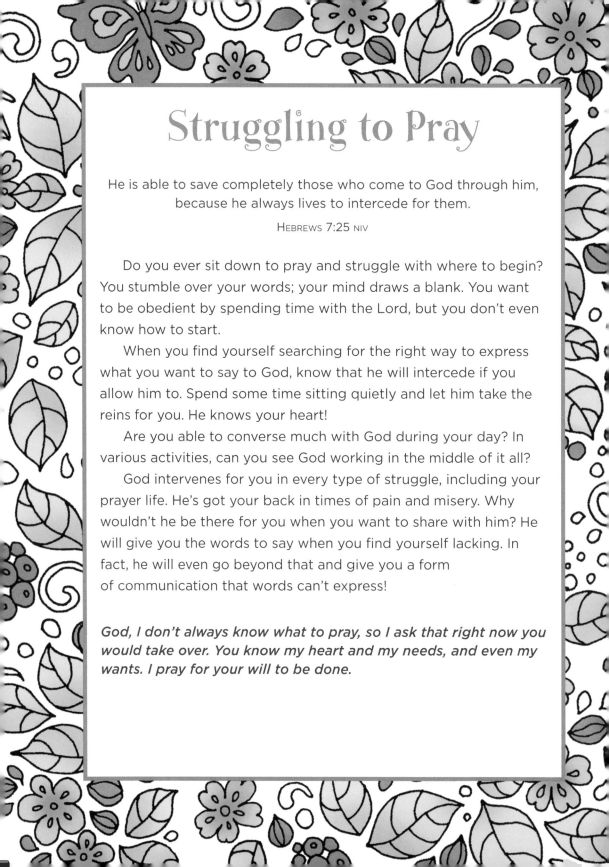

Struggling to Pray

He is able to save completely those who come to God through him, because he always lives to intercede for them.

HEBREWS 7:25 NIV

Do you ever sit down to pray and struggle with where to begin? You stumble over your words; your mind draws a blank. You want to be obedient by spending time with the Lord, but you don't even know how to start.

When you find yourself searching for the right way to express what you want to say to God, know that he will intercede if you allow him to. Spend some time sitting quietly and let him take the reins for you. He knows your heart!

Are you able to converse much with God during your day? In various activities, can you see God working in the middle of it all?

God intervenes for you in every type of struggle, including your prayer life. He's got your back in times of pain and misery. Why wouldn't he be there for you when you want to share with him? He will give you the words to say when you find yourself lacking. In fact, he will even go beyond that and give you a form of communication that words can't express!

God, I don't always know what to pray, so I ask that right now you would take over. You know my heart and my needs, and even my wants. I pray for your will to be done.

He is able to
save completely
those who come to
God through him,
because he always
lives to intercede
for them.

Hebrews 7:25 NIV

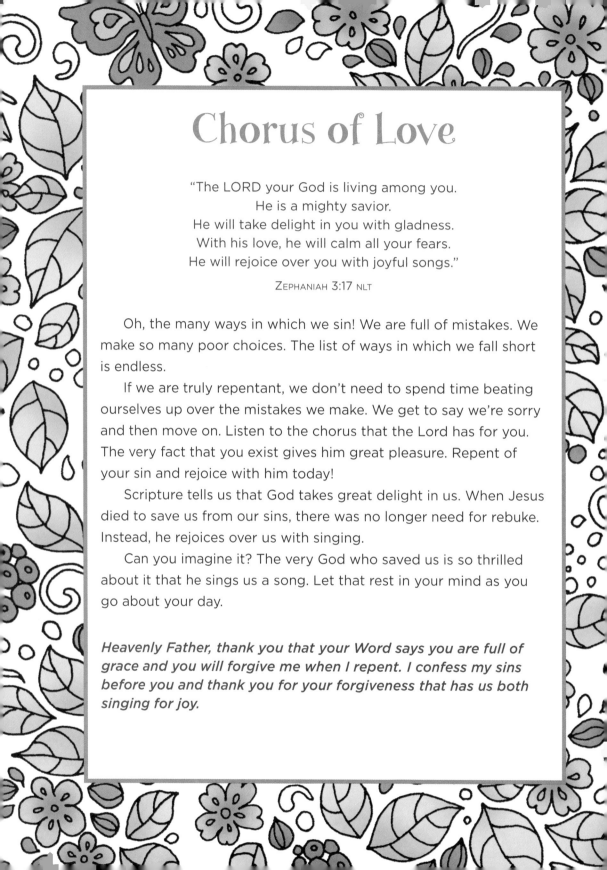

Chorus of Love

"The LORD your God is living among you.
He is a mighty savior.
He will take delight in you with gladness.
With his love, he will calm all your fears.
He will rejoice over you with joyful songs."

ZEPHANIAH 3:17 NLT

Oh, the many ways in which we sin! We are full of mistakes. We make so many poor choices. The list of ways in which we fall short is endless.

If we are truly repentant, we don't need to spend time beating ourselves up over the mistakes we make. We get to say we're sorry and then move on. Listen to the chorus that the Lord has for you. The very fact that you exist gives him great pleasure. Repent of your sin and rejoice with him today!

Scripture tells us that God takes great delight in us. When Jesus died to save us from our sins, there was no longer need for rebuke. Instead, he rejoices over us with singing.

Can you imagine it? The very God who saved us is so thrilled about it that he sings us a song. Let that rest in your mind as you go about your day.

Heavenly Father, thank you that your Word says you are full of grace and you will forgive me when I repent. I confess my sins before you and thank you for your forgiveness that has us both singing for joy.

He will take delight in you with gladness. With his love, he will calm all your fears. He will rejoice over you with joyful songs.

Zephaniah 3:17 NLT

Toxic Thinking

This righteousness is given through faith in Jesus Christ to all who believe. There is no difference between Jew and Gentile, for all have sinned and fall short of the glory of God.

ROMANS 3:22-23 NIV

Sometimes while driving, little annoyances can spur us into a prideful mindset: we're the only ones driving at a safe speed, or signaling correctly, or paying attention to the rules of the road. *Why doesn't anyone else know what they're doing?* Small things escalate quickly, and suddenly we're out of control, figuratively speaking. It's pride, plain and simple. *I have it all figured out, and everyone else needs to get with it.* This kind of thinking is not only unpleasant for those around us, but it's toxic to the soul. And it spreads quickly!

It's best to set your mind on Christ and his reconciliation and set it quickly before you start condemning friends and family too! We're all just doing our best to get where we need to go. We're not superior to anyone, and we're not too terrible either because God created us and sent his Son to die for us. This makes us worthy.

Think about this verse today whether you're on the road or not. Pray you'll arrive safely wherever you're going, and maybe try a pleasant wave to others on the way there.

Think about the wonderful, merciful gift of God tonight and thank him for making you right with him through that gift.

God, I know sometimes I am judgmental of other people. Give me a pleasant attitude toward others. I have experienced your forgiveness, so I choose to forgive others who have hurt me. Give me grace as I deal with those around me.

Enemy Tactic

Let all who take refuge in you rejoice;
let them ever sing for joy,
and spread your protection over them,
that those who love your name may exult in you.

Psalm 5:11 esv

The more you dive into your relationship with the Lord, the more the enemy will want to pull you away. The more you begin to listen for God's voice, the more Satan will try to whisper in your ear. Allowing yourself to become closer to God is the last thing the enemy wants for you.

You're not good enough. Nothing is going right for you. You're making all the wrong decisions. These lies may play over and over again in your head until they start to sound like reality. Suddenly, you find yourself believing them. This isn't what God wants for you! He wants you to be glad in him. Make sure you are listening to the right voice.

Many thoughts pass through your mind each day. As you weigh them against Scripture, are they words that give you joy and make you sing? Those are the words that you need to hold on to.

Pray for protection from the lies the enemy wants you to believe. Ask the Lord to speak in a voice that is loud enough to hear through the deception. He wants to rejoice with you; he wants what's best for you. Trust in that knowledge as you spend time with him.

Lord, thank you for giving me wisdom to know what is truth and what are lies from the enemy. Continue to help me filter those thoughts and dwell on your words that give me joy.

Application Accepted

He chose us in him, before the foundation of the world, to be holy
and blameless in love before him.

EPHESIANS 1:4 CSB

Applications are essential for gleaning the promising applicants
from the inadequate. Fill out this form and find out if you're
approved for a home loan, for college admittance, for a credit card.
We put our best qualities on paper, tweak our weaknesses, and
hope for approval. But rejection is always a possibility.

With God, however, our acceptance has already been promised.
We must only appeal to his Son, Jesus, who steps in on our behalf
and petitions for our approval. There is no credit flaw, no failing
grade, and no past default that his death on the cross doesn't
redeem completely.

Because we are covered with God's loving forgiveness, there
is no flaw in us. We are accepted by him as part of his family and
redeemed by his grace for his eternal kingdom.

Can you believe your acceptance? Stand on the promise that
there is nothing in your history—no past or present sin—that can
separate you from his love. Cast everything upon him and have
faith; you are wholly accepted and abundantly loved!

*Thank you, Jesus, for redeeming all humanity, so I can live in this
new life and hope that tells me my sin is forgiven. I want to walk
closely with you. Help me to walk in holiness today, which is only
possible with you!*

He chose us in him, before the foundation of the world, to be holy and blameless in love before him.

Ephesians 1:4 CSB

A Strong Oak

In their righteousness, they will be like great oaks
that the LORD has planted for his own glory.

Isaiah 61:3 NLT

How many thoughts does the human brain conceive in an hour? In a day? In a lifetime? How many of those thoughts are about God: who he is and what he has done for his children? Imagine your own thoughts about life—grocery lists, dentist appointments, song lyrics, lost keys—and your thoughts about God—his majesty, holiness, comfort, creativity—weighed against each other on a scale. Likely, it would tip in favor of the many details of human existence.

These temporary details overshadow the one comfort and promise we can rely on: the gospel of Jesus' birth, death, resurrection, and ascension for our eternal salvation. Wipe every other thought away, and we are left with this truth. For those burdened by their sin it is of great comfort. Jesus came to give us new life!

You are not a weak sapling, limited by inadequate light and meager nourishment. You are a strong and graceful oak, soaring and resilient for the glory of God. Ashes and mourning and heavy burdens are relieved.

The scales tip to this one weighty thought: you are his. Let your thoughts stretch above the canopy of everyday human details to bask in this joy. He has given you everything you need.

Father God, thank you that in those times of deepest need, you are the water of life that I can draw my strength from. Help me to drink deeply of your living water today.

Never-ending Joy

"The LORD has filled my heart with joy;
I feel very strong in the LORD.
I can laugh at my enemies;
I am glad because you have helped me!"

1 SAMUEL 2:1 NCV

Consider for a moment the most joyous time of your walk with Christ. Imagine the delight of that season, the lightness and pleasure in your heart. Rest in the memory for a minute, and let the emotions come back to you. Is the joy returning? Do you feel it? Now, hear this truth: the way you felt about God at the highest, most joyful, amazing, glorious moment is only a fraction of how he feels about you all the time!

What a glorious blessing. Our joy is an overflow of his heart's joy toward us; it is just one of the many blessings God showers on us. When we realize how good he is, and that he has granted us everything we need for salvation through Jesus, we can rejoice!

The season of your greatest rejoicing can be now, when you consider the strength God provides, the suffering from which you have been rescued, and the rock that he is.

His blessings don't depend on you feeling joyous; you experience joy because you realize God's gracious and loving blessings. Lift your praises to him and let your song be never-ending.

God, you have made me strong. Thank you that I don't have to worry about who I might face today. I have you right next to me, rescuing me from all unrighteousness.

A Worthy Friend

My soul, bless the LORD,
and do not forget all his benefits.
He forgives all your iniquity;
he heals all your diseases.
He redeems your life from the Pit;
he crowns you with faithful love and compassion.

PSALM 103:2-4 CSB

God created you for relationship with him just as he created Adam and Eve. He delights in your voice, your laughter, and your ideas. He longs to fellowship with you just as he did with his first son and daughter.

The friendship God offers is a gift of immeasurable worth. There is no one like him; indeed, there is none as worthy of your fellowship than God Almighty, your Maker and Redeemer. Train your heart to run first to him with your pain, joy, frustration, and excitement. His friendship will never let you down.

When life gets difficult, do you run to God with your frustrations? When you're overwhelmed with sadness or grief, do you carry your pain to him? In the heat of anger or frustration, do you call on him for freedom?

God is a friend who offers all this to us—and more—in mercy and love. He is worthy of your friendship. Talk to him tonight before you go to sleep. He loves to hear from you.

God, help me to see your goodness all around me today. Let me notice it in the small things and in the big things. Thank you for making me whole.

My soul,
bless the Lord,
and do not
forget his benefits.
He crowns you with
faithful love
and compassion.

Psalm 103:2, 4 CSB

Unending Chorus

Creation itself will be set free from its bondage to corruption and obtain the freedom of the glory of the children of God.

ROMANS 8:21 ESV

Some days begin with praise on our lips and a song in our hearts. Humility covers us like a velvet cloth, soothing and delicate and gentle. The truth of God plays on repeat: "God is good! God is good! I am free!" and the entire world's darkness cannot interrupt the chorus.

But other days begin by fumbling with the snooze button and forfeiting the chance to meet him in the quiet stillness. Pride is a sneaky companion, pushing and bitter and ugly, and we wonder if we will ever delight with God again. We feel bound.

Do you know how much God wants you to rest in his presence? He is waiting and faithful and tender. The ups and downs should be familiar by now, perhaps, but can you ever become accustomed to the holy living side-by-side with your flesh? One glorious day, flesh will give way to freedom, and there will be no side-by-side. Only the holy will remain. And we will sing the unending chorus of God's goodness as we sit before his heavenly throne.

When you spend time with God, there is no need to hide. You can be exactly who you are. There is freedom in his presence. Feel that freedom now.

God, give me perspective about my day and even my week. Remind me that my life is important but eternity is better!

True Satisfaction

My dove in the clefts of the rock,
in the hiding places on the mountainside,
show me your face,
let me hear your voice;
for your voice is sweet,
and your face is lovely.

SONG OF SONGS 2:14 NIV

Stress threatens to get the better of us, and sometimes we just want to hide. Remembering that secret bar of chocolate in the pantry, we may scurry off to bury ourselves away with the temporary comfort that helps the world slow down if only for a moment.

The same instinct can arise with God. We get overwhelmed by his ministry or overdue for his forgiveness or out of touch with his Word and lose track of who he is. Instead of running toward him, we hide from him and look for other ways to meet our needs.

You cannot outrun God's love for you, nor should you try. Instead, leave the false safety of the clefts and crannies and pantries with hidden chocolate. Feel the pleasure of his friendship. This God who wants to hear your voice and see your face because he finds them sweet and lovely is waiting for you.

Is there anyone else who can satisfy you so perfectly? Let him see you tonight.

Lord Jesus, I don't need to hide from you, but I get so caught up in my day I often forget to see that you are a part of it. Call out to me above the busyness and the noise, and I will come to you.

Show me your face, let me hear your voice; for your voice is sweet, and your face is lovely.

Song of Songs 2:14 NIV

A Whisper

A great and strong wind tore the mountains and broke in pieces
the rocks before the LORD, but the LORD was not in the wind.
And after the wind an earthquake, but the LORD was not in the
earthquake. And after the earthquake a fire, but the LORD was
not in the fire. And after the fire the sound of a low whisper.

1 KINGS 19:11-12 ESV

We often want, more than anything, to go the distance for God.
Our deepest desire is to sacrifice for him no matter the cost. But
what we don't always realize is that past the sacrifice, past the
actions, and past the gifts, God really just wants our hearts.

We strain to hear from God, and we expect his answer in a
thunderous clap; we search for him in a firestorm. But when we
are at the end of ourselves, down on our knees before him, then
he will speak in that still small voice that we have to be broken and
humbled to hear.

We know the character of God, but we still look for him to act
outside of it on a daily basis. We know that he is after our hearts,
but we seek to give him more because we fear, deep down, that our
hearts won't be enough.

God speaks in a whisper because he wants to reveal to us that
he isn't about the show. He just wants us to love him. Can you hear
his whisper today?

*God, I face a busy day with a lot of noise and other things trying
to grab my attention. As I quiet my heart before you, speak to me
and allow me to hear your gentle whisper.*

Sometimes,
God speaks in a
whisper.

Truly Special

You are a chosen people, a royal priesthood, a holy nation,
God's special possession, that you may declare the praises of
him who called you out of darkness into his wonderful light.
Once you were not a people, but now you are the people of God;
once you had not received mercy, but now you have received mercy.

1 PETER 2:9-10 NIV

We all want to believe that we are special. Most of us grow up being told that we are, and it feels good to believe it. But over time we look around and realize that, really, we are just like everyone else. Doubt begins to creep in, making us second guess ourselves and damaging our self-confidence.

Long before you were even a wisp in your mother's womb, you were set aside and marked as special. You were chosen to be God's special possession, and that's pretty amazing.

God sees you as special. Revel in that knowledge right now. He is calling you out of the darkness of the ordinary and bringing you into the light of the extraordinary.

God picked you. He loves you. He wants you. Trust in that and let it change the way you think about yourself.

God, help me to accept that I am special and chosen. Give me confidence that I can make an influence in this world even today because you have chosen me to be in this place for a purpose.

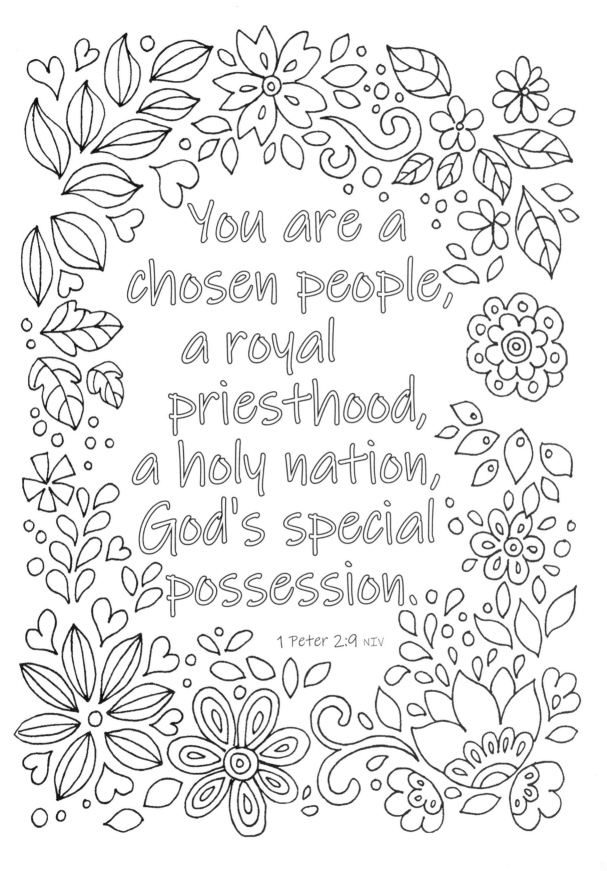

You are a chosen people, a royal priesthood, a holy nation, God's special possession.

1 Peter 2:9 NIV

He Gets It

Since we have a great high priest, Jesus the Son of God,
who has gone into heaven, let us hold on to the faith we have.
For our high priest is able to understand our weaknesses.
He was tempted in every way that we are, but he did not sin.

HEBREWS 4:14-15 NCV

One of the most beautiful things about the God we serve is that he knows exactly what we are going through at any given time. How does he know? Because he has been there himself.

When Jesus came to earth in the form of a human, he was tempted by the same everyday things we are. Whether it's lust, unkind thoughts, or unwarranted anger, he had to face it. Just like we do.

You can bring your temptation and confessed sin to the Lord without fear; he knows exactly how you're feeling. He is not some far off God in the sky who cannot relate to you and your life. He walked on the earth, and he saw and felt the struggles you feel.

Pray for protection from temptation, just as he did, and he will answer you.

Thank you, Jesus, that you can relate to my weakness. Thank you for going to the cross for my weakness and wearing it yourself, so I can have newness of life in you. Help me to resist temptation and live for you.

Son Before the Sun

In the morning, having risen a long while before daylight,
He went out and departed to a solitary place; and there He prayed.

MARK 1:35 NCV

When do you find time to pray? Even if you are intentional and passionate about prayer, everyday activities almost always take priority over time with God. It is often said that prayer can happen at any time, and of course it does, but is there value in setting aside a specific time to communicate with the Lord?

Did you ever realize that the notion of quiet times comes from the example set by Jesus? He would get up before daylight and pray in a solitary place. About what, no one is sure. It's not the content that matters; it's the willingness to maintain our relationship with the Father and seek his will.

Instead of trying to fit prayer into your busy day, pray before it gets busy, so you can cope with the pressures of life. Can you find a solitary place to hear from God? Now is your time!

Be like Jesus and find the time and space to sit with the Father. You will find more joy and peace when you have the right frame of mind from the beginning of the day.

Jesus, I give you this moment. Thank you for the opportunity to spend quiet time with you.